HOW TO
COMMUNICATE
EFFECTIVELY

HOW TO COMMUNICATE EFFECTIVELY

ASHISH SINGH

ASSOCIATE PROFESSOR
MBA AGRI BUSINESS
RAJIV GANDHI SOUTH CAMPUS

BANARAS HINDU UNIVERSITY

PARTRIDGE
A Penguin Random House Company

To order additional copies of this book, contact
Partridge India
000 800 10062 62
www.partridgepublishing.com/india
orders.india@partridgepublishing.com

TABLE OF CONTENTS

CHAPTER I

Communication

Introduction

Imagine the life without conversing with anyone. In school times, we all must have read Robinsons Crusoe tales. He was alone on the island for very long time. But there also, he was conversing with animals. That is, he found way to converse.

Thus in short, it can be said that man is social animal. This means that any living being, be it person or an animal will always try to live in close proximity of other entities. Living in close proximity of others is not the end. There is always need of sharing something with other persons—be it some happy new, be it some sort of anger, be it sad news or anything. There comes the need for communication of ideas with other person.

Communication may be defined as the process involving transferring information from one entity to another. Thus, the process always involves two entities—one who is sender and other who is receiver. The sender sends the information through some means, which is called channel in technical terms, while the receiver receives the information, send by the sender. Without the presence of these two entities, communication is not possible in any case. Have you ever imagined someone talking to himself/herself? In flowchart form, communication can be understood as follows

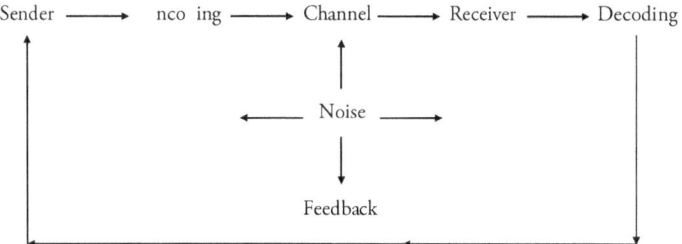

Elements of communication

Sender: One who wishes to send ideas to other entities. It may be a person, or animal or an organization. And one thing is always to be remembered. No communication is possible without the presence of sender. He/she is essential element of communication process.

Encoding: The ideas which have to be communicated are not clearly visible to other entities e.g. those ideas may be in the minds of sender. Thus, these ideas have to be translated into a form which can be transmitted using some sort of channel. This may include saying the ideas, or writing the ideas etc.

Channel: It refers to any mechanism used for transmitting encoded ideas to the receiver. It can be air, or a computer, or a paper etc. Without the presence of channel, no communication is possible. If you remember one thing studied in school—no communication is possible in vacuum. Vacuum means absence of any channel of communication.

Receiver: It is the second entities that receive the encoded ideas. It can be once again the person, or animal, or an organization. Again, no communication is possible without the presence of receiver. H e/she is second essential element of communication process.

Decoding: It refers to understanding of message sent by sender. It depends on the psychology of the receiver. And obviously, it occurs on the part of receiver. Another thing to be remembered is that in practice, hundred percent understanding of idea or message sent by sender is not possible. In other words, this is root cause of noise (or sometimes called as gateways or barriers to communication process).

Feedback: It is the essential part of any communication process. It is again sending the response to the sender. In a way, it is reverse communication process i.e. it occurs from receive to the sender. The feedback can be either positive or negative. If the message was interpreted in the way it should have been, the feedback is positive or else it is negative.

Noise: If the feedback is negative, then there are some elements which are causing the feedback to be negative. These undesirable elements are called as noise. They are also sometimes called as gateways or barriers to communication process. They reduce the effectiveness of communication. Their presence ensures that the receiver is not fully understand the meaning of sender message. And once again, noise is present to some extent in the communication process. To reduce it is the foremost task of any communication manager.

Nature of Communication

There are many nature of communication as the subject and practical thing. One thing has to be kept in mind by all the readers. Nature, feature and characteristic of any subject, including communication, are one and same thing. There is no difference between the three. The nature of communication is as follows:

1. It depends on at least two entities. One of them as to be sender and other one receiver. If only one entity is present, communication cannot occur. The sender cannot communicate to no one. Receiver cannot receive the message if there is no sender. Thus both the parties must be present for communication to take place.

2. In practical sense, feedback is essential for communication process. Without it, one cannot understand whether the communication was correctly understood by the receiver or not. In practice, feedback can be return message from the receiver, or it can be behavior of receiver, or it can be as simple as nodding of head from the receiver. It is up to sender to understand it.

3. On this very note, communication is best, when it is two way. That is, both the entities are free to

communicate with each other. This also removes any doubt present in the communication process. In short, it is best if ideas are sent from the sender and feedback is received from the receiver.

4. In practice, there is some element of noise present in communication process. That is, full understanding of message is not possible in practical terms. There can be many reasons for the same. They are discussed later in chapter.

Purpose of communication

As already stated, man is a social animal. Thus, he/she communicates with other entities with any of the following purpose:

1. Information purpose: One main purpose is to give and take information with other entities. It can take the form of notice, or it can be in the form of pamphlets etc. Main objective to give information and nothing else.

2. Giving orders: Giving orders is a crucial aspect of any organization and this purpose takes place between superior and subordinate. For any task, orders are given to specific subordinate.

3. Giving reports: After completion of orders, reports are given and this takes place between subordinate and superiors. One thing has to be remembered—giving reports is the process of giving feedback.

4. Social needs: Again it needs to be stressed that man is a social animal and he/she is in need of satisfying their social needs. There communication comes into

play. He/she communicate to satisfy their social obligations.

5. Need for persuading: Many times we wish to persuade others about what we think is correct. There arises the need for communication. We wish to convince others about the things we believe are correct.

CHAPTER II
Types of Communication

Communication type

Organizational communication can be of many types depending on the level of authority of both sender and receiver. This level of authority is set by the organization concerned. The type of communication can be:

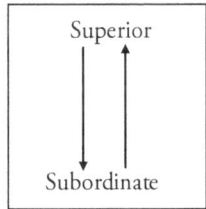

1. Vertical communication:—It occurs when the authority of sender and receiver are different but their department is same. For example, a manager and sales person of marketing department are communicating with each other.

   It can be of two types:

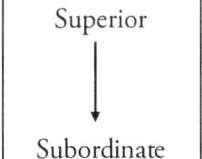

   Downward communication: When orders are given in organization, they flow in downward direction i.e. from higher authority (superior) to lower authority (subordinate).

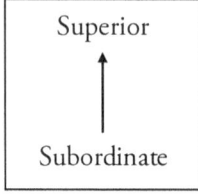

Upward communication: When orders are fulfilled or unfulfilled, they are reported and the direction is upward i.e. from lower authority (subordinate) to higher authority (superior).

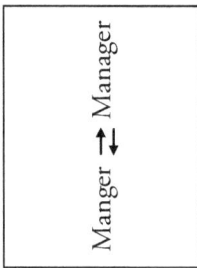

Department I

2. Horizontal communication:—This communication occurs between persons at same authority level. For example, managers of two departments say for example marketing and finance departments are communicating with each other. It can be friendly chat, office matter etc.

Department I

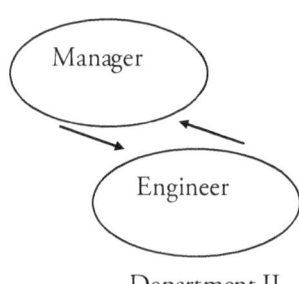

Department II

3. Diagonal communication: It occurs between persons at different authority levels and in different departments too. This is a major difference from vertical communication. For example, manager from marketing departments is communicating with engineer from production department.

Formal and information communication

If we talk of business communication, it is necessary to discuss formal and informal communication. By formal means that thing which is formally declared. In business sense, it is declared by the organization. Formal communication can be defined as that communication which is created by the organization and which controls it. For this purpose, organization creates some authority and responsibility. This communication flows along the lines of authority. If you remember, we had discussed the concept of downward, vertical, diagonal communication etc. They are all forms of formal communication.

Informal means just the opposite. It is not declared formally. It is created by some other means other than organization. Informal communication is also present in all business organization. It is created by some other forces rather than organizational factors. Those other forces are factors related to social and psychological factors of human beings. For example, two persons of different department are good friend. Being a good friend is outside the control of organization. The two persons form a group which is informal. And one more thing has to be mentioned. The size of formal group is within the control of organization. But the size of informal group is not within the control of organization. It can be small or large, but in any case, it is beyond the control of organization.

Grapevine—side effect of informal group.

As discussed earlier, informal communication is beyond the control of any organization. Thus, it can be the root cause of true messages or untrue messages. If it is cause to untrue messages, then in business terms, it is called as grapevine. And there is reason behind it. As the vine of grapes grow anywhere without and control, in the same way, untrue messages can pass to any person without any control.

These grapevines are normally called as rumors. It is up to organization to control them and to utilize them effectively. One thing needs to be mentioned. It cannot be eliminated fully.

An organization can utilize these grapevines in some cases. They are as follows:

1. If a communication has to be transmitted quickly, then grapevine is best. It travels lot faster than formal communication.
2. If things have to be molded from organization point of view, grapevine is best for that purpose.

In short, it is best to reduce the grapevines. And is some particular cases, it can be utilized effectively.

CHAPTER III
Barriers to Effective Communication

Barriers to effective communication

As mentioned earlier, there is some element of noise present in the communication process, no matter how much effective it is. These noises render some portion of communication ineffective. These noises are also called as barriers to communication process or gateway to communication. They are called as gateway due to very special reason. In home, gate is installed to prevent entry by default. The same reason can be applied to communication process also. They prevent effective communication process—that is, they prevent total grasping of sender message and they also prevent sending of feedback.

Thus the study of gateway or barrier is important. If it is studied, then attempt may be made to reduce them. And one thing is most important and once again may be stressed—it is not possible to completely remove the noises. Some element of noise will remain. In practical situations also, we all must have experienced the barriers to communication.

This barrier to communication is much easily understood if it is broken down into parts. The parts of communication barriers are as follows:

Organizational barriers

1. Lack of communication facilities.
    Some organizations do not have all the communication facilities required by the people. This creates problem in sending the message or in receiving the feedback. Some of the latest communication facilities, which may be absent may be video conferencing, internet access through Wi-Fi etc.
2. Closed door policy.
    Some organizations or some people within that organization are not so much open to communication and consider it as waste of time. This is closed door policy. This makes the sending of message and receiving of feedback very difficult.

Physical barriers

1. Channel disturbances
    Sometimes communicates gets distorted due to some problem in channel. We all face temporally dead phones, sometimes the communication through mobile fails due to network congestion etc. They all are due to channel disturbances.

2. Absence of same communication facilities at both the ends
    Ever tried sending message through internet to a person residing in a village? Never because you know that the receiver will not be having computer and internet connection at his or her place. Thus, the communication requires normally that both the sender and receiver to have same equipments to facilitate the communication process. If this is absent, this may be a barrier to communication.

Personal Barriers

1. Personal distrust
    Sometimes both the parties engaged in communication process distrust each other. Thus, may not convey true message or accurate feedback to the other parties. This is normally due to perception.
2. Lack of confidence
    Sometimes the sender is having serious doubts about the level of confidence in the receiver. Thus he/she ignores the communication or sends incomplete communication to the receiver. In either case, it is a barrier to communication process.
3. Lack of time
    Some persons in the organization are so busy that they find no time to communicate with others. This is also gateway to communication process.
4. Underestimating importance of communication
    Some people do not understand the important role communication plays in the life. They simply ignore the communication process on the whole.

Semantic barriers

1. Language differences
   Sender and the receiver may be different in the sense that they speak different languages. This is very serious gateway to the communication process. The true meaning of sender message and the feedback is not known to both the parties.
2. Different cultures
   The cultures of both the parties may be different. This particula.rly assumes more importance in the case of non verbal communication. In Japan, shaking of hands will seem inappropriate because they have a tradition of bowing to each other. In India, younger people touch the feet of elderly people. But in Western countries, this will mean surrender.
3. Not understood by the receiver
   Many a times, receiver does not understand the full meaning of the sent message. Thus, feedback received from him/her is incomplete. This is barrier to communication process.

Overcoming barriers to effective communication

First thing to be understood is that it is not possible to make communication process noise free. There will be at least some barriers to the communication process which act as gateway to communication. But it is true that barriers to communication should be minimized. There are some methods of doing so. They are as follows:

1. Treat the other party respectfully. The element of respect should be present. If it is absent, barriers in form of psychological elements will appear.
2. Try to discover the underlying elements of the other party culture. This becomes more important if the other party culture is quite unknown to us. If this is not done, barriers in form of cultural differences will arise.
3. There should be common ground of topic of communication and both the sender and receiver should agree to it.
4. Try to minimize physical barriers to communication. For example, if the receiver is not having particular equipment, then either provides that equipment or use common equipment available to both the parities.
5. Never underestimate the importance of communication. If you feel, then one can hold workshop on the same.
6. If language is problem, we can obviously take help of translator.

CHAPTER IV
Essential components of Communication

Seven C's of communication

It is quite popular in management to describe any event by using some alphabet. For example, in marketing, 4 P's are used to describe marketing mix. And this method is quite simple and easy to understand.

In the same lines, 7 C's of communication are described, which denotes features of effective communication. They are as follows:

1. Completeness
    The communication must be complete in itself. It should convey all ideas and facts required by the receiver. The sender of the message must take into consideration the receiver's mind set and convey the message accordingly.

2. Conciseness
    Conciseness means wordiness. In other words, communicating what is to be conveyed in least

possible words. Conciseness is a necessity for effective communication.

3. Consideration

   Consideration implies "stepping into the shoes of others" or it can be called as empathy. Effective communication must take the audience into consideration. Make an attempt to visualize the receiver and also ensure that the self-respect of that person is maintained.

4. Clarity

   The sender should be absolutely clear about what he/she wants to communicate. He/she should be clear about what he/she wants the receiver to understand.

5. Concreteness

   Concrete communication implies being particular about the idea rather than fuzzy and general. It refers to using data and information for conveying correct messages. Concreteness strengthens the confidence.

6. Courtesy

   Courtesy in message implies the message should show the sender's expression and should also maintain the respect to the receiver. The sender of the message should be sincerely polite, judicious, reflective and enthusiastic.

7. Correctness

   Correctness in communication implies that there are no grammatical in communication. And one thing has to be noted—it is applicable to all the languages.

It is advisable to keep all the seven C's into consideration to make the communication process more effective and fool proof.

CHAPTER V
Writing the Letter

Introduction

In normal situations and in the business world, writing letter is the most common medium of communication. In practical terms, giving letter in writing is considered more legally safe than oral speaking. Thus this section of book will deal with intricacies involved in writing the correct letter, in order to get the feedback desired from the receiver.

Advantages of writing the letter

As mentioned earlier, letter is considered more valuable in the court that oral speaking. But that is in the case off controversies. In general, letter has many other advantages.

They are as follows:

1. Writing the letter gives more chances of getting the desired response from the receiver. It is considered more effective from the receiver end.

2. Letter has got legal validity. If some legal case is done, letter can be produced as a evidence in the court.
3. It gives chances of storage of the letter. If one copy is stored in the office, then the same can be produced anytime for any other purpose. This is a definite advantage over oral speaking.
4. Writing the letter targeted to one receiver gives more chance of adopting the letter for that particular receiver only. Thus, the same letter can be modified little bit to suit that particular receiver only.

Disadvantages of writing a letter

The letter writing has got numerous advantages over oral speaking. But, that is one side of a coin. The other side has many disadvantages too. They are as follows:

1. Writing a letter involves some cost, which includes cost of stationery, cost of computer and its accessories, cost of sending the letter etc. Thus, the letter writing has got many advantages, but at the cost.
2. Immediate feedback is not possible in this form of communication. You have to wait some time before getting the feedback. And that time may be quite short or might be very long.
3. If there is some problem at receiver end in understanding that letter, getting the clarification from the sender involves time.
4. Storing one copy of letter in the office involves some office space, along with cost. So, that letter can be used at the legal document, but again at cost.

5. Some receivers are so passive that they will exactly the same, as has been mentioned in the letter, without modifying some of the things. In such cases, one has to be very careful in writing the letter.
6. If the letter has to be sent to many receivers, then the cost involved is quite large. It will involve the cost of photo copying and the cost the sending the letter to many receivers.

But whatever may be advantages or disadvantages, the letter has always assumed prominent place in the business communication.

So, the next few chapters of this book will deal with letter writing in detail.

CHAPTER VI
Parts of letter

Introduction

If you are writing personal letter to any one near and dear to you, that letter may in any format. But if that letter is writing for business purpose, to someone in the organization, then, that letter should be in proper format.

By proper format means that the font size, line spacing, location of left paragraph, location of right paragraph, various portions of that letter and their relative positions etc. should be predefined and should not change. So, this chapter deals with this aspect of the letter writing, particularly with parts of letter.

Portions of a letter

Any business letter has some specific portions, which are as follows:

1. Letter Head:—This portion is specific for each organization and it includes the name of that organization, address of organization, phone numbers, e-mail address, web site address, name of sender, designation of that sender, specific telephone number and e-mail address of that sender and finally a particular logo of that organization. It can be shown in the following figure:

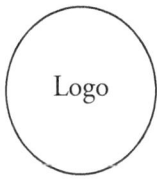

XYZ Company Ltd
Full Postal Address
Phone number & Fax number
E-mail address

Mr. ABC
Designation
Phone number
E-mail address

---

2. Reference number and Date:—It includes the specific reference number for that particular letter (it can be organization place, year, the particular category of receiver sent and the letter number). This reference number is used in the future for getting the letter retrieved. Also, the date of writing the letter is also included.

| Logo | XYZ Company Ltd
Full Postal Address
Phone number & Fax number
E-mail address |

Mr. ABC
Designation
Phone number
E-mail address

Ref. No.: XYZ/Mumbai/Misc/01   Date: DD/MM/YYYY

3. Inside Address:—It includes the name of the receiver, along with full postal address of the place where the receiver is situated.

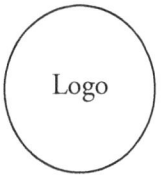 XYZ Company Ltd
Full Postal Address
Phone number & Fax number
E-mail address

Mr. ABC
Designation
Phone number
E-mail address

Ref. No.: XYZ/Mumbai/Misc/01   Date: DD/MM/YYYY

To,
Mr. EFG,
Designation,
Full postal Address

---

4. Subject Line:—This is very essential element of business letter and it shows the crux of the letter. It has to be included in every business letter.

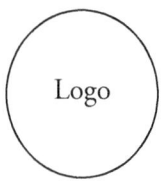

XYZ Company Ltd
Full Postal Address
Phone number & Fax number
E-mail address

Mr. ABC
Designation
Phone number
E-mail address

Ref. No.: XYZ/Mumbai/Misc/01   Date: DD/MM/YYYY

To,
Mr. EFG,
Designation,
Full postal Address
Sub:— _____

5. Salutation:—This is a courteous way to start any letter. It may be Dear Sir/Madam, or Respected Sir/Madam or simply Sir/Madam. But it has to be included in any business letter.

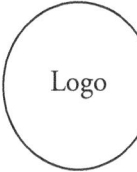
XYZ Company Ltd
Full Postal Address
Phone number & Fax number
E-mail address

Mr. ABC
Designation
Phone number
E-mail address

Ref. No.: XYZ/Mumbai/Misc/01   Date: DD/MM/YYYY

To,
Mr. EFG,
Designation,
Full postal Address
Sub:— _____
Sir/Madam,

6. Contents of that letter:—This is the main part of that letter. It is normally divided into three portions—introduction, main contents and the conclusion. After that, it is customary to write thank you in every business letter.

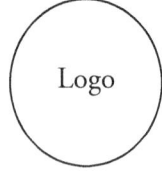

XYZ Company Ltd
Full Postal Address
Phone number & Fax number
E-mail address

Mr. ABC
Designation
Phone number
E-mail address

Ref. No.: XYZ/Mumbai/Misc/01   Date: DD/MM/YYYY

To,
Mr. EFG,
Designation,
Full postal Address
Sub:— _____
Sir/Madam,
Introductory Paragraph
Main Contents
Conclusion Paragraph
Thank you,

7. Senders name:—After that, the sender name is written along with some salutation along with some space for signature.

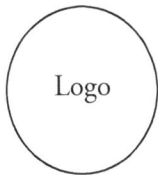 XYZ Company Ltd
Full Postal Address
Phone number & Fax number
E-mail address

Mr. ABC
Designation
Phone number
E-mail address

Ref. No.: XYZ/Mumbai/Misc/01   Date: DD/MM/YYYY

To,
Mr. EFG,
Designation,
Full postal Address
Sub:— _____
Sir/Madam,
Introductory Paragraph
Main Contents
Conclusion Paragraph
Thank you,

Closing salutation,
Signature
(Mr. ABC)

8. Enclosure:—If anything of interest to receiver is to be included in the letter, it is mentioned in the list of enclosure. It is an optional thing, which can be omitted, if not desired.

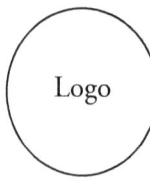

XYZ Company Ltd
Full Postal Address
Phone number & Fax number
E-mail address

Mr. ABC
Designation
Phone number
E-mail address

Ref. No.: XYZ/Mumbai/Misc/01   Date: DD/MM/YYYY

To,
Mr. EFG,
Designation,
Full postal Address
Sub:— _____
Sir/Madam,
Introductory Paragraph
Main Contents
Conclusion Paragraph
Thank you,

Closing salutation,
Signature
(Mr. ABC)

Encl:
1.
2.
3.

9. Copy to:—If so desired, the letter is sent to some other persons, normally for information or for information and necessary action. If either the list of enclosure is attached or copy to is attached, or both of them, one signature at the end.

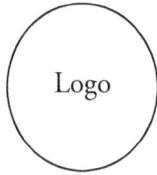 XYZ Company Ltd
Full Postal Address
Phone number & Fax number
E-mail address

Mr. ABC
Designation
Phone number
E-mail address

Ref. No.: XYZ/Mumbai/Misc/01   Date: DD/MM/YYYY

To,
Mr. EFG,
Designation,
Full postal Address
Sub:— _____
Sir/Madam,
Introductory Paragraph
Main Contents
Conclusion Paragraph
Thank you,

Closing salutation,
Signature
(Mr. ABC)

Encl:
1.
2.
3.

Copy to: For information/information and necessary action.
1.
2.

(Mr. ABC)

10. P.S.:—If anything in the letter is not written forgetfully, then it is normally include in the P.S. column. This is also a optional part.

(Logo)

XYZ Company Ltd
Full Postal Address
Phone number & Fax number
E-mail address

Mr. ABC
Designation
Phone number
E-mail address

Ref. No.: XYZ/Mumbai/Misc/01   Date: DD/MM/YYYY

To,
Mr. EFG,
Designation,
Full postal Address
Sub:— _____
Sir/Madam,
Introductory Paragraph
Main Contents
Conclusion Paragraph
Thank you,
Closing salutation,
Signature
(Mr. ABC)

Encl:
1.
2.
3.

Copy to: For information/information and necessary action.
1.
2.

(Mr. ABC)

P.S.:— _____

That completes the business letter in proper format.

CHAPTER VII
Formats of Business Letter

Introduction

As already mentioned, every business letter has its own format. This format goes on changing a little bit. This chapter of book is dedicated to this aspect of business letter.

There can be lot of format of business letter. But overall, this format can be classified into two types—block form and indented form. These two portions will be discussed in detail in comi.ng parts.

Block form of letter writing

In this form, all the paragraphs are justified from left hand margin and right hand margin. This form is also sometimes called Full Block Form. The illustration is given below:

```
_____

XYZ Company Ltd                      ╭─────────╮
Full Postal Address                  │         │
Phone number & Fax number            │  Logo   │
E-mail address                       │         │
                                     ╰─────────╯

Mr. ABC
Designation
Phone number
E-mail address
_____
Ref. No.: XYZ/Mumbai/Misc/01        Date: DD/MM/YYYY

To,
Mr. EFG,
Designation,
Full postal Address
Sub:— _____
Sir/Madam,
Introductory Paragraph
Main Contents
Conclusion Paragraph
Thank you,
Closing salutation,
Signature
```

(Mr. ABC)

Encl:
1.

Copy to: For information/information and necessary action.
1.

(Mr. ABC)
P.S.:— _____

All the paragraphs are from the left hand margin and they are also justified at the right hand margin.

Semi Block form

This letter is quite similar to above mentioned letter with the only difference that the closing salutation is on the right hand side. Rest all the things are the same.

XYZ Company Ltd
Full Postal Address
Phone number & Fax number
E-mail address

Logo

Mr. ABC
Designation
Phone number
E-mail address

Ref. No.: XYZ/Mumbai/Misc/01   Date: DD/MM/YYYY

To,
Mr. EFG,
Designation,
Full postal Address
Sub:— _____
Sir/Madam,
Introductory Paragraph
Main Contents
Conclusion Paragraph
Thank you,

                     Closing salutation,
                          Signature
                          (Mr. ABC)

Encl:

1.

Copy to: For information/information and necessary action.
1.

(Mr. ABC)

P.S.:— _____.

This is just a slight modification of full block style.

Indented Style

As is clear from the name, all the opening lines of paragraphs are indented from the left hand side of margins. The closing salutation is also on the right hand side.

	XYZ Company Ltd
Logo	Full Postal Address
	Phone number & Fax number
	E-mail address

Mr. ABC
Designation
Phone number
E-mail address

Ref. No.: XYZ/Mumbai/Misc/01   Date: DD/MM/YYYY

To,

      Mr. EFG,

      Designation,

      Full postal Address

Sub:— _____

Sir/Madam,

      _____

_____

      _____

_____

      _____

Thank you,

Closing salutation,
Signature
(Mr. ABC)

Encl:

    1.

Copy to: For information/information and necessary action.

    1.

(Mr. ABC)

P.S.:— _____.

Hanging Indent form

This is slight modification of indented form. In this, all the first line of paragraphs start at the left hand margin while the remaining lines start at indented form. This style of letter writing is not so prevalent in the business world.

XYZ Company Ltd
Full Postal Address
Phone number & Fax number
E-mail address

Logo

Mr. ABC
Designation
Phone number
E-mail address

Ref. No.: XYZ/Mumbai/Misc/01   Date: DD/MM/YYYY

To,
Mr. EFG,
Designation,
Full postal Address
Sub:— _____
Sir/Madam,

_____
_____
_____
_____
_____
_____

Thank you,

Closing salutation,
Signature
(Mr. ABC)

Encl:
1.
Copy to: For information/information and necessary action.
1.

(Mr. ABC)

P.S.:— _____.

CHAPTER VIII
Different types of letter

Having discussed the different formats of letter, we are in the position to discuss some types of letter written in business world. The main objective is to get desired response from the receiver without offending him/her. So, ne thing is very crucial—be courteous in every letter, be it a complaint letter.

Now we will discuss different types of letter.

Sales letter

The main objective of sales letter is to get sales done, which is the ultimate aim of any organization. But getting money out of customer's pocket is next to impossible thing. Thus, this letter is written with ultimate care and caution.

The objective behind this letter can be many, which include:
1. To make customers aware about the product or service.
2. To get telephone appointment.
3. To get face to face appointment.
4. To get the sales done.

To get an edge over the numerous sales letters received by any customer, some rules have to be followed. They are as follows:

1. The sales letter has to be personalized. It has to be written according to need of every customer.
2. It has to be relevant and no part of that letter should be useless i.e. it should focus on the product or service only.
3. To gain the attention of customers, there should be use of statement or headline, related to that product or service.
4. The time required for gaining the attention is shrinking day by day. This is most probably because of increasing competition, resulting in more sales letter received by individual customer.
5. The letter should say something about your organization, how effective and efficient you are with respect to that product or service.
6. It should be credible i.e. every part of that letter should be trustworthy.
7. If possible, keep the sentences short. Too long sentences make the letter difficult to understand.
8. The letter should be written in perfect grammar.
9. Last but not the least, the sales letter should be grammatically perfect.

In maximum cases, the sales letter should be written using AIDA approach—an age old approach which is still relevant today.

1. Attention—grab it using some attractive opening statement or headline.
2. Interest—gain it using some interesting facts about your product or service.

3. Desire—impart it into your customer by using lucrative terms like discounts, free gifts etc.
4. Action—Convince the customer to act immediately.

Some additional points have to included in the sales letter. They are as follows:

- Headline or commonly called banner statement should be included in the letter. They create more interest in the minds of customer.
- Credibility statement should be included in every letter. They ensure the credibility in the minds of every customer.
- How and Why statements should be included in the letter which explains why your product or service is better than the competitors and what are different outlets for buying that product or service.
- Action statement is required to explain the benefits of buying that product or service at the earliest.

Sample sales letter is given in the following section:

Smart Mobile Phone—not another mobile phone

Dear Mr. XYZ,

Full postal address

Your organization is very big one catering to thousands of clients everyday. Imagine carrying y.our laptop and the mobile every day? There has to be a solution.

Our organization has developed a mobile phone, especially for clients like you, which has got the features of mobile, tablet and a laptop.

We work with accomplished craftsmen that use state of the art, modern machines which enhance the clarity of our phones, and give them an award winning style. They will never fail you in the network clarity, battery life is so long that it can be called as infinite, it covers all the features of tablet and laptop and above all, it comes with a three year warranty. What more can you ask in a mobile phone?

If you purchase this exclusive mobile phone within 15 days, you will get a Bluetooth, manufactured by the same company absolutely free of cost and a discount of 10% immediately.

We are waiting eagerly for you at the exclusive mobile store. Hope that you will not miss this *chance of a lifetime*.

Thanking you in anticipation of early visit,

Yours Faithfully,

(Mr. ABC)

Marketing Manager

P.S.: If you find it difficult to visit the store, please call us and we will arrange a demo for you in the place of yours convince.

Quotation Letter

This letter is written to bid against a particular item(s). This letter includes the name of item(s), price and the special terms and conditions, if any. A sample letter for quotation is shown below:

Paper Company Ltd
2, Nariman Point, Mumbai
Ph. No. 022-00000000,
Fax no. 022-111111111
E-mail address: XYZ@XYZ.com

Logo

Mr. EFG
Marketing Manager
Phone number: 022-222222222
E-mail address:ABC@XYZ.com

R.ef. No.: Paper/Mumbai/Quot/01   Date: 12/12/2013

To,

Mr. ABC,

Production Manager,

XYZ Company Ltd.

21, Santa Cruz, Mumbai

Sub:—Quotation for 10 reams of paper.

Sir,

We are submitting the quotation for 10 reams of paper of A4 size Executive Bond paper. We are quoting a price of Rs. 150 per ream of paper. We will be requiring 50% part payment with the order letter, if this quotation is passed.

Thank you,
Yours Faithfully,
Signature
(Mr. EFG)

Order Letter

This letter is very simple to place an order before the receiving organization. All the terms related to that order are mentioned in the letter like description of item, number of units sought, any special features to be included etc. Date at which you expect the order to delivered at the door is also mentioned.

Sample order letter is given below:

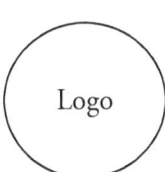

XYZ Company Ltd
21, Santa Cruze, Mumbai
Ph. No. 022-00000000,
Fax no. 022-111111111
E-mail address: XYZ@XYZ.com

Mr. ABC
Production Manager
Phone number: 022-222222222
E-mail address:ABC@XYZ.com

Ref. No.: XYZ/Mumbai/Misc/01   Date: 01/01/2014

To,
Mr. EFG,
Marketing Manager,
2, Nariman Point, Mumbai
Su.b:—Order for 10 reams of paper.

Sir,

We require 10 reams of paper of A4 size Executive Bond at the organization latest by 15/01/2014. We are enclosing a part payment cheque and the rest will be on delivery of the order.

We expect the same level of quality that you have been famous for.

Thank you,

Yours Faithfully,

Signature

(Mr. ABC)

Complaint letter

As it prominent from the name itself, this letter is written to lodge a complaint about anything, which can be quality not delivered, less quantity delivered, time delay in receiving an order, regarding financial misconduct of the organization etc.

Letters of complaint usually include the following stages:

1. Background
   This section describes the situation, which is causing some concern at the organization.
3. Problem
   This portion contains the actual problem, which is of concern to the organization. It may be less quantity received, quality is not up to the mark, delay in receiving the order or anything.
5. Effect
   The effects of that problem on the organization are also mentioned. It may be production delay, delay in fulfilling the orders of customers, quality is not up to the mark etc.
4. Solution
   The solution is always mentioned because mentioning a problem without suggestion is always treated as incomplete. It may be make up the shortfall immediately, correcting the invoice or any other solution.
5. Warning
   It is always advisable to put a light warning note at end of letter. It may be looking at other sources of supplies, legal action, late payment fees etc.

6. Closing

At the closure of this letter, it is again advisable to close with a hope that the receiving organization will sort out the matter. It can be "I look forward to receiving your explanation of these matters", "I look forward to receiving your payment", "I look forward to settle this matter" etc.

The tone of complaint letters should not be aggressive or insulting, as this would definitely annoy the receiving organization and not encourage them to solve the problem.

The sample complaint letter is given below:

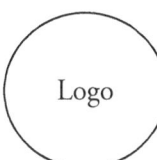

XYZ Company Ltd
21, Santa Cruze, Mumbai
Ph. No. 022-00000000,
Fax no. 022-111111111
E-mail address: XYZ@XYZ.com

Mr. ABC
Production Manager
Phone number: 022-222222222
E-mail address:ABC@XYZ.com

Ref. No.: XYZ/Mumbai/Comp/02   Date: 17/01/2014

To,
Mr. EFG,
Mar.keting Manager,
2, Nariman Point, Mumbai
Sub:—Complaint regarding Order for 10 reams of paper.

Sir,

We have ordered 10 reams of paper of A4 size Executive
Bond at the organization latest by 15/01/2014. We have also
enclosed a part payment cheque. This was done on the belief
that your organization is fulfilling the orders promptly.

But, it is very sorry to state that the order was not delivered
on time, and the whole production process was delayed due
to this. This has created a bad impression on the customer,
without any fault by own.

If this thing is continued later on also, we will have no option other than to look for other supplier.

Thank you in anticipation of further correction,

Yours Faithfully,

Signature

(Mr. ABC)

Cover Letters

A cover letter is a document sent with resume to provide an insight or overview into information on your skills and experience.

A cover letter typically provides detailed information on why the sender is qualified for the job to which he/she is applying for. An effective cover letters explain the reasons for sender interest in the specific organization and identify the most relevant skills or experiences, which makes him/her more suitable for the job.

The sample cover letter is shown below:

Date: 01/01/2014
To,
Mr. XYZ,
Human Resource Manager,
ABC Company Ltd.,
21, Nariman Point,
Mumbai
Sub: Application for the post of Marketing Executive.

Dear Sir,

I am applying for the post of Marketing Executive as advertised in the Ascent dated 25/12/2013. The experience and skills you need for the job match me.

I worked for DEF Company as Marketing Assistant for 2 years and then moved on the MNO Company as Marketing

Executive, where I am still working. The same can be verified from. two companies.

I am enclosing herewith my resume and testimonials for your kind perusal.

Looking forward to meeting you to further discuss the things.

Thank you,

Yours Sincerely,

(ASH)

The covering letter is slightly changed if it is for a non experienced sender. The sample letter in shown below;

Date: 01/01/2014
To,
Mr. XYZ,.
Human Resource Manager,
ABC Company Ltd.,
21, Nariman Point,
Mumbai
Sub: Application for the post of Marketing Executive.

Dear Sir,

I am applying for the post of Marketing Executive as advertised in the Ascent dated 25/12/2013.

I have just passed my Master of Business Administration from Banaras Hindu University, with CGPA 8.25. I have been always interested in the field of Marketing Executive.

In fact, I have also done my summer training and project dissertation of somewhat related topic.

I am enclosing herewith my resume and testimonials for your kind perusal.

Looking forward to meeting you to further discuss the things.

Thank you,

Yours Sincerely,

(ASH)

One thing has to be remembered. The cover letter is written on plain paper without the use of letter pad. It is the sender alone who is applying for the job, not the whole organization.

But, it is essential to send the resume in both the cases. Without it, the cover letter has got no value. Preparation of resume will be discussed in the later parts of this book.

Information Seeking Letter

This letter is written by the sender who wishes some information regarding anything from the organization. That information can be related to price of that product, job vacancy in the organization etc.

The sample letter is shown in the following lines:

Date: 01/01/2014

To,
Mr. XYZ,
Human Resource Manager,
ABC Company Ltd.,
21, Narim.an Point,
Mumbai
Sub: Seeking the information about the vacancy.

Dear Sir,

I am come to know that there are some vacancy of Marketing Executive lying vacant in your esteemed organization.

I have just passed my Master of Business Administration from Banaras Hindu University, with CGPA 8.25. I have been always interested in the field of Marketing Executive.

In fact, I have also done my summer training and project dissertation of somewhat related topic.

If it is so, please inform me of the same so that I can also apply for it.

Looking forward to your letter

Thank you,

Yours Sincerely,

(ASH)

This, and many other letters are written to and between the organizations. But one thing has to be kept in mind—that is politeness. If the tone of the letter is not polite, that letter is useless in every terms, and will not fulfill the objective of getting the desired response from the receiver.

CHAPTER IX
Preparation of Resume

Introduction

In the last chapter, it was mentioned that cover letter is complete without the preparation of resume. So, in this chapter, we are going t.o discuss about the different type of resume and their preparation.

Now, resume gives the detailed insight into the academic qualifications, work experience, personal details, some references etc. It is prepared for the receiver to let him/her judge your suitability for the job; i.e. matching the features of job with the features you possess.

The resume format can vary. It is up to you to decide which format to follow. But, the main thing is that resume are meant for the receiver of the organizations. Thus, it is advisable to remain as simple as possible, keeping all the things into consideration.

Format of Resume

Resume format is of general types and it covers the following points:

1. Name
2. Designation: The designation of the person is also given. This part is optional because the resume is also prepared for that person, who is not engaged anywhere. So, in that case, resume does not contain the designation.
3. Address: It contains the full postal address of the sender, and it has the permanent and the current address of the sender. In addition, it contains phone number(s), email address and the website, if any of the sender.
4. Job at which where he/she is working: This part contains the name of organization, designation, and the brief about his/her duties and responsibilities. This part is again optional, and may be excluded for those who are not engaged anywhere.
5. Past Work Experience:—This part contains the past records of work experience which includes name of organization, tenure of working in that organization, designation and the brief about his./her duties and responsibilities. This part is again optional.
6. Education Profile: This part contains all the education records of the sender. It includes name of examination passed, year of passing, University or Board associated, and the marks or grade obtained.
7. Other related profile: It may include the details of conferences, seminars, workshop, etc., if they are

associated with the job. It is again optional, and may be added, if the sender has some.

8. Awards: This portion includes some awards and medals, if there are, which is mentioned in this section. This part is optional, and may be included, if desired.

9. Personal Details: It includes details like name of father, date of birth, marital status, languages known etc.

10. References: This portion is quite crucial since it contains the name of two or three persons, who are very well convers.ant with the sender, and belong to either education line or working line or both. Full postal address along with telephone numbers, email address and designation is also given. It is very important because the hiring organizations feel it relevant to check the previous character of the person who they are thinking of taking. Second, the designation and the organization of references plays a very important role, in the process of current selection.

11. Name of sender, place and date of sending along with signature is the last portion of the resume.

In addition, some latest formats of resume also include the place of photographs, or the address of website, for further references, or a link to a video for further information etc.

But, the things that have been mentioned above are very crucial for forming a correct resume.

Some sample resume are given below:

I) For sender without any job experience: This is the case of persons without any job, or without any job experience. In such cases, the work experience column is eliminated and other things remain the same.

The sample resume is shown below:

Photograph

Resume
Mr. ABC
R111, Santa Cruze
Mumbai—841001
Ph. No. 022-11111111
Mob. No. 9999999999
Email: abc@resume.com

Educational Qualification:—

1. Passed Master of Business Administration from XYZ University, Mumbai in 2013 with 80% marks.
2. Passed Bachelor of Engineering from DEF University, Pune in 2011 with 75% marks.
3. Done 10+2 from GHF school, Mumbai in 2007 with 75% marks.
4. Done 10th from GHF school, Mumbai in 2005 with 70% marks.

Awards:

1. Got a certificate from GHF school in 2007 for getting 100 marks in Mathematics.
2. Got a certificate from GHF sch.ool in 2005 for doing a social work.

Personal Details:

Father's Name: Mr. JKL.
Date of birth: 11th April 1987
Marital status: Unmarried
Languages known: English, Hindi
Strengths: Friendly, extroverts
Weakness: Impatient for the work to be done.

References:

1. Mr. CVB,
   Assistant Professor
   XYZ University
   Mumbai
   Ph. No. 022-22222222
   Email address: cvb@mygmail.c.om

2. Mr. ASD,
   Assistant Professor
   DEF University
   Pune
   Ph. No. 024-22222222
   Email address: asd@mygmail.com

Date: 01/01/2014   (ABC)

Place: Mumbai

II) For senders with job Experience: In this case, work experience is also added with current objective. Rest all the things remain approximately the same.

Resume

Mr. ABC
Marketing Executive
OPL Company Ltd.
R222, Santa Cruze
Mumbai—841001
Ph. No. 022-11111111
Mob. No. 9999999999
Email: a.bc@resume.com

[Photograph]

Objective

To work in the field of marketing so well so as to raise my company to the first position.

Work Experience

1. Working as Marketing Executive in OPL Company Ltd. since 2013. Basic responsibilities include adding new customers, satisfying old customers, getting feedback etc.
2. Worked as Marketing Assistant in HJL Company Ltd. from 2012-2013 where I was responsible for getting new customers.

Educational Qualification:—

1. Passed Master of Business Administration from XYZ University, Mumbai in 2011 with 80% marks.
2. Passed Bachelor of Engineering from DEF University, Pune in 2009 with 75% marks.
3. Done 10+2 from GHF school, Mumbai in 2005 with 75% marks.
4. Done 10th from GHF school, Mumbai in 2003 with 70% marks.

Awards:

1. Got a certificate from GHF school in 2005 for getting 100 marks in Mathematics.
2. Got a certificate from GHF school in 2003 for doing a social work.

Personal Details:

Father's Name: Mr. JKL.
Date of birth: 11th April 1987
Marital status: Unmarried
Languages known: English, Hindi
Strengths: Friendly, extroverts
Weakness: Impatient for the work to be done.

References:

1. Mr. CVB,
    Assistant Professor
    XYZ University
    Mumbai
    Ph. No. 022-22222222
    Email address: cvb@mygmail.com

2. Mr. ASD,
    Marketing Manager
    OPL Company Ltd.
    Mumbai
    Ph. No. 022-22222222
    Email address: asd@mygmail.com

Date: 01/01/2014   (ABC)
Place: Mumbai

This is the basic two types of resume. The formatting can be of any type, depending upon the sender preferences and the organization to which it is sent.

CHAPTER X
Communication regarding the meeting

Introduction

Every organization is having meeting now and then. In the formal meetings, there is a procedure for conducting the meeting. This procedure has to be followed every time one has to hold a meeting.

Every meeting starts with a notice to all the members, which is given at least seven days in advance by the secretary of the committee. This notice is given well in advance so that, if any member wishes to put agenda in meeting, he/she has got enough time is prepare for it.

After this, agenda is prepared which is list of all the points to be discussed at the meeting. The notice and agenda are prepared well in advance of meeting.

After this, meeting is held, and all the points, which are resolved in that meeting is recorded in the form of minutes. These minutes is also prepared by the secretary and given to all the members after completion of meeting.

Thus, the communication regarding the meeting is divided into three parts—notice, agenda which are prepared before the meeting and minutes which are prepared after completion of meeting.

Now, all the three things will be discussed in detail in following sections.

Notice

As mentioned earlier, the notice is the first point in any meeting. The notice regarding the meeting contains some points like name of committee, date of meeting, time of meeting and place of meeting.

This notice, as discussed earlier, is given at least seven days in advance.

Sample notice, regarding the meeting, is given below:

	XYZ Company Ltd
Logo	21, Santa Cruze, Mumbai
	Ph. No. 022-00000000,
	Fax no. 022-111111111
	E-mail address: XYZ@XYZ.com
	Mr. ABC

Secretary

Phone number: 022-222222222

E-mail address: ABC@XYZ.com

Ref. No.: XYZ/Mumbai/Meeting/01   Date: 01/01/2014

Notice

All the members of Advisory Committee are hereby informed that a meeting will be held on 09/01/2014 at 1100 hours in the Committee Room of the Administrative Block. All are requested to attend the same.

(Secretary)

Some points may be noted for the sample notice given above. First, the notice is given well in advance of the date of meeting. Second, there is no need of any wishes or informal conversation in the notice. Only, straight points are written, ignoring all the informal points. Third, the notice contains the name of committee (in this case, it is Advisory Committee), date of meeting (in this case, it is 09/01/2014), time of meeting (in this case, it is 1100 hours) and the place of meeting (in this case, it is Committee Room of Administrative Block).

Agenda

The next point to be decided is the agenda of meeting. It is simply a list of all the points to be discussed at the meeting. As a customary measure, all the points, discussed in the notice are once again in the agenda. The agenda is also circulated well in advance to all the members, so as to give them some time to think over the points and to discuss the same, during the meeting.

Sample agenda is shown below:

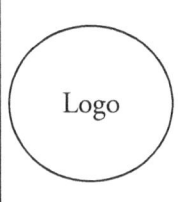

XYZ Company Ltd
21, Santa Cruze, Mumbai
Ph. No. 022-00000000,
Fax no. 022-111111111
E-mail address: XYZ@XYZ.com
Mr. ABC

Secretary
Phone number: 022-222222222
E-mail address: ABC@XYZ.com

_____

Ref. No.: XYZ/Mumbai/Agenda/01   Date: 02/01/2014

Agenda

A meeting will be held on 09/01/2014 at 1100 hours in the Committee Room of the Administrative Block. The agenda regarding the same is as follows:

1. To discuss the increase of price of commodity X in the market and the side effect, if any.
2. To consider the rise of salary of the employees and to decide the level to which it should be increased.
3. To consider launching of new product Y, whose trial run has been completed successfully.

(Secretary)

These two communications are done before the meeting date, well in advance.

Minutes

This is the third communication, which is done after the completion of the meeting. It lists all those points that were resolved at the meeting, and is signed again be the secretary.

The sample minutes is shown below:

	XYZ Company Ltd
(Logo)	21, Santa Cruze, Mumbai
	Ph. No. 022-00000000,
	Fax no. 022-111111111
	E-mail address: XYZ@XYZ.com
	Mr. ABC

Secretary
Phone number: 022-222222222
E-mail address: ABC@XYZ.com

Ref. No.: XYZ/Mumbai/Minutes/01   Date: 10/01/2014

Minutes

A meeting was held on 09/01/2014 at 1100 hours in the Committee Room of the Administrative Block, Chaired by Mr. H. The minutes regarding the same are as follows:

Members present:

Mr. H	:	Chairman
Mr. U	:	Member
Mr. D	:	Member
Mr. E	:	Member (In absentia)

Mr. ABC   :   Secretary

The Chair welcomed all the members and passed the minutes of previous meeting.

1. The committee resolved to increase the price of commodity X in the market by 5%. But, it will provide the edge to the competitors. So, there has to be more advertisement on televisions and newspapers also. It was decided to increase the advertisement budget by 2%.
2. It was resolved that due to rising inflation, salary of employees should be increased. The Daily Allowance portion has to increased by 5%.
3. It was resolved by the committee that launch of new product should be postponed to festival Holi to gain immediate increase in sales.
4. With special permission of Chair, Mr. U raised the issue of sick leave. It was resolved that 5 sick leave per year may be given to employees.

After that, the meeting was ended, with vote of thanks by the Chair.

(Secretary)

Some points may be noted for the minutes.

1. It is customary to write the note of welcoming by the Chair to all the members.
2. It is also customary to write that minutes of previous meeting were passed.
3. It is essential to write names of members present in the meeting and names of members absent from the meeting.
4. It the end, it is customary to give vote of thanks by the Chair.

CHAPTER XI
Report Writing

Report is a brief description of current situation, also called as problem, and a set of suggestions, that can be taken to resolve that problem. It is always informative and fact based i.e. it contains all the points related to some point or another, and these points are based on some facts.

Some key features of the report are as follows:

1. Information and fact-based are essential feature of any report.
2. All the reports are formally structured. All the points are decided well in advance and they are fixed in the structure. That structure cannot be changed.
3. It is always written with a specific purpose and made according to the audience.
4. It is written according to style appropriate to each part and it can also include part headings
5. It uses bullet points, number and tables or graphs for better clarity.
6. It includes suggestions or recommendations for action.

What makes a report bad?

There are some points that make a good job seems bad. They are as follows:

1. Badly structured report is of no use for anybody. A report should be in proper format for better understanding.
2. An inappropriate writing style makes the job look like worse.
3. Incorrect or no referencing of the used material from any other source makes a report looks bad.
4. Too much or too little or irrelevant material makes the reader bored and should be avoided.
5. In worst part, a report does not relate results to purpose for which it has been created.
6. Using too much long sentences or unnecessary use of jargon makes the report difficult to understand.

How to ensure that report is a good report?

Some points may be checked to ensure this. They are as follows:

1. Does it answer the purpose in the brief? Does it give solution to the problem?
2. All the materials has been placed in the appropriate sections?
3. Has all the data been checked for accuracy? Are the data not too old?
4. Graphs and tables have been carefully labeled?
5. Graphs and tables are also explained in words?

6. Does the discussion and conclusion and the objectives match?
7. Is some data irrelevant?
8. Is the report written in appropriate style, suited for the readers?
9. Is it jargon-free, long sentences free and clearly written?
10. Has every idea taken from other source been acknowledged with a reference?
11. Have all illustrations and figures taken from other source been acknowledged?
12. Has the report been carefully proof-read?

If these points are carefully been taken care off, then the report is bound to be very good.

Contents of report

Every report has some contents, placed in a particular order. This order should never be changed, and should be kept as it is. These contents are as follows:

1. Executive Summary: The executive summary includes a brief summary of the key points. The executive summary should include a summary of all parts of the report including recommendations. Without recommendations, the executive summary has got no purpose.
2. Contents: The contents page of the report contains the chapter, unit number and the page number.
3. Introduction: The introduction page says why the report is being written. Reports are always written to solve a business problem. Reports maybe be

started because there is a crisis or it is written on routine matter.

4. Findings: This information is not always read by reader, but it is important. Without thorough research and consequent analysis, the report does not have any meaning. Also if anything in the executive summary surprises the reader, then they will definitely read this portion of the report.

5. Conclusions: The conclusions portion summarizes the findings section but does not include diagrams or graphs in this area. This area should be short, clearly follow the order of the findings and lead naturally into the recommendations, and should be numbered or bulleted.

6. Recommendations: Report is never completed without the recommendations or suggestion page. That is the main crux of the report.

7. Bibliography: It contains list of all books, journals, articles, newspapers, magazines, internet addresses etc. used for writing the report. That portion is very important from legal point of view.

8. Appendices: It may include the questionnaire, or any other material, not included in the report, but in which the reader may be interested.

CHAPTER XII
Verbal Communication

Introduction

Till so far, everything that have been discussed revolves around written communication. Be it letter, or communication related to meeting, or resume—they are all written communication. That is only one part of communication.

Second part is related with verbal communication. That implies, communicating with others using oral medium. So, this section briefly describes ways and means of improving the oral communication, in order to get more chances of getting right response.

Definition

In this case, the information or message is communicated orally without use of written medium. It may mean exchange of words between two or more persons or use of audio-video device.

It may include speeches, presentations, discussions, and all the aspect of interpersonal communication. The main advantage is getting the immediate feedback from the receiver.

Advantages

Oral communication offers great advantages to both sender and receiver. They are as follows:

1. Getting instant feedback. I am a teacher and get immediate feedback from the students. Some papers are very easy, and the feedback is strongly positive. Other papers are little bit harder, and the feedback is not positive. Thus, this communication medium implies immediate feedback from the sender.
2. Sender has got the opportunity of making the communication more simple, if the feedback received is not positive. So, in my class, I get the chance of delivering the lecture is slightly different way, if the feedback is not positive.
3. Very low cost of communicating is present in this case. If you are addressing a big gathering, even then, cost incurred is of audio system. So, the cost is approximately nil.

Disadvantages

Oral communication has some disadvantages too. They are as follows:

1. Oral communication has got no legal validity. That is, it cannot be produced as legal evidence.
2. In the case of addressing big gatherings, some of the receivers give negative feedback. But, it is quite

possible that they might be ignored by the sender, because of not noticing them.

But still, oral communication has got its importance in the field of communication. That will be discussed in coming sections.

How to make oral communication more effective

Oral communication is developed as a conscious effort. There are some ways to improve it. They are as follows:

1. Develop a habit of reading. It will help you to increase your vocabulary, help you express ideas in variety of ways etc.
2. Before speaking, think a little bit about the words. Using too many words will result to severe downfalls, which include boring your listeners, take too much time and may result in credibility failure.
3. Prepare if you have time. Writing skills are much easy rather than oral communication. In oral communication, there is no second chance.
4. Listen more and talk less. This will allow the speakers to be also involved in communication.
5. Be aware of non-verbal communication. It is very big part in oral communication—words, their tone, the gestures you make, facial expressions and body language you use, your posture, your eye contact are all included in this.
6. Honesty is the best policy. Be sure about whatever you say. Never speak anything which is not possible in practical situation. If the receiver catches a little bit wrong in your presentation, he/she is bound to teat whole presentation wrong.

7. Show and seek some understanding from the receivers. And the best way is to look at receivers and try to notice something like nodding of head, listening carefully or something like that. In the class which I take, if the receiver ask some questions, it means that they are interested. If nobody asks a questions, then my whole lecture goes waste.

8. Think about receiver perspectives. In other words, it can be said that "putting yourself in other shoes". What you are saying is suited to you, but not necessarily to the receiver.

If these things are brought into practice by the sender, then he/she will surely enhance the skills of his/her verbal communication.

CHAPTER XIII
Non Verbal Communication

Introduction

Till so far, everything that have been discussed revolves around written and verbal/oral communication. Be it letter, or communication related to meeting, or resume, presentation, interview etc.—they are all written or oral communication. That is only part of communication.

Another part is related with non verbal communication. That implies, communicating with others using non verbal messages. Have you ever observed the ways in which a mother communicates with her baby? That is the effectiveness of non verbal communication. The communication done by deaf and mute persons is other example of non verbal communication.

So, this section briefly discusses the method of non verbal communication and the various mechanisms used in it.

Non verbal communication messages

The way of sitting, way of standing, way of moving the hands, eye contact frequency, facial expression, silence etc. are ways and means of communicating non verbally. They are also used to increase the effectiveness of oral communication.

The various mechanisms used are as follows:

1. Way of sitting: The way in which you sit is indicator of your interest in the communication.

Each sitting ways describes different interest in the speaker and the receivers tuning.

2. Way of standing:—While giving presentation or while entry into the room, the way in which the person enters creates the *first impression* in the mind of receiver. That is it is old saying that the way you enter an interview room, decides whether you will be selected or not.
3. Communicating with fingers or hand:—This is another way of communicating with other person using symbols drawn with hand. Have you ever noticed the sign of *V* after winning the match?

This shows a very effective way of communication, without talking.

Each visual represents a different case—for victory, for lift, for pointing out, raising a question, for fighting etc. But, the main and crucial thing is that there is no need to utter any word in the sequence.

4. Pictorial representations: In almost of the countries, a picture is placed before everything written in their language. If you are not able to understand their language, you can easily interpret the things from the picture.

Some pictures are shown below:

Telephone

Workshop

Restaurant

Bar

Sport Complex

Handicapped

No Smoking

Railway

Taxi Stand

Airport

Ship yard

Post Office

5. Silence:—Silence is the lack of any audible sound inaudible to any human being. In other words, the silence can also refer to any absence of communication, according to many experts. But some other says that silence is also *a total communication*.

If we talk of nonverbal communication, it can mean many different things. Some things are as follows:

 i)   Complete understanding.
 ii) Complete confusion.
 iii) Agreement.
 iv) Disagreement.
 v)   Passive nature.
 vi) Thinking of something else.
      Etc.

So in brief, communication is broadly of three types:

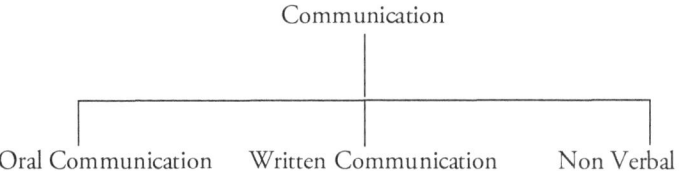

All these parts have been discussed in detail in previous sections. They must be very clear to you.

www.ingramcontent.com/pod-product-compliance
Lightning Source LLC
Chambersburg PA
CBHW072039190526
45165CB00018B/1174